Language Builders

Nathan and Nicole Learn about
NOUNS

by Ann Malaspina
illustrated by George Hamblin

Content Consultant
Roxanne Owens
Associate Professor, Elementary Reading
DePaul University

NORWOOD HOUSE ☐ PRESS
CHICAGO, ILLINOIS

Norwood House Press
P.O. Box 316598
Chicago, Illinois 60631
For information regarding Norwood House Press, please visit
our website at:
www.norwoodhousepress.com or call 866-565-2900.

Editor: Arnold Ringstad
Designer: Jake Nordby
Project Management: Red Line Editorial

Paperback ISBN: 978-1-60357-701-4

The Library of Congress has cataloged the original hardcover
edition with the following call number: 2014030272

Manufactured in the United States of America in North
Mankato, Minnesota.
262N—122014

Words in **black bold** are defined in the glossary.

People, Places, and Things

My new camera is amazing! This week, I'm snapping photos of nouns. Sound strange? It's my teacher Miss Gomez's idea. She says that a noun names a person, place, or thing. After that, nouns get a little confusing. Miss Gomez wants me to use my camera to take pictures of nouns.

Tomorrow, I'm taking the camera on our class trip to the Statue of Liberty. Nicole's aunt, Mrs. Smith, is coming along as a chaperone. "Look out for nouns on Liberty Island!" Mrs. Smith said. <u>Statue</u> is a noun. So is the word <u>island</u>. Nouns are everywhere. You just have to keep your eyes open. See, Miss Gomez, I'm catching on!

Since she writes awesome poems, Nicole is taking her fancy pen. Maybe she'll write a poem with lots of nouns. There's one thing I still haven't figured out. Miss Gomez said, "Not all nouns can be photographed." What did she mean by that? It's a noun mystery. Maybe I can solve it on Liberty Island.

By Nathan, age 9

Nicole and Nathan's class trip to the Statue of Liberty got off to a rough start. It was a windy day in New York Harbor. The ferry bobbed in the waves, making everyone feel seasick.

"Let's look for nouns for our assignment," said Nicole. "Maybe we won't feel so queasy."

Nathan aimed his camera at a sailboat. "I see three nouns! *Sailor*, *sea*, and *waves*." He took several pictures.

Nicole scribbled on her notepad. "Those are common nouns. They name any person, place, or thing," she said. She was a talented poet, and she was looking forward to writing poems about the field trip.

The sail lifts in the wind
like a bird's wing,
taking us on a journey
with the waves.

Whoosh! A gust of wind rocked the boat. Nicole's hat flew off her head.

"Catch Nicole's hat!" yelled Nathan.

It was too late.

Nicole's aunt, Mrs. Smith, turned toward Nathan. She had come along as a chaperone. "Did you know that *Nicole's* is a **possessive** noun?" she asked.

"I remember! A possessive noun shows who owns something. Nicole owns her hat," said Nathan.

"Not anymore!" said Nicole.

"All sentences need a noun," added Mrs. Smith. "Most sentences have two or more."

"Don't nouns have different jobs?" asked Nathan.

"That's right," said Mrs. Smith. "One job is to be the subject of the verb."

Nathan said, "The verb is the action, so the noun must be the subject that is related to the action."

"*Nathan snaps photographs. Nathan* is the person who is snapping," said Nicole.

"What about *photographs*? Isn't that a noun, too?" asked Nathan.

"Yes. It's the direct object of the verb. The photographs are being snapped," said Mrs. Smith.

Everyone thought about nouns. They looked across the choppy water to the skyscrapers in the city.

"New York City is a very special place," Nicole said, taking notes.

"It's also a proper noun. Names of people, places, or special things are proper nouns," said Nathan. "Remember, these nouns start with capital letters."

Everyone thought of proper nouns.

"Central Park!" said Mark.

"The Statue of Liberty!" said Lynn.

"Miss Gomez!" everyone said at once.

Nathan snapped some photos.

Nicole wrote a poem.

Miss Gomez is a proper noun and so are Lynn and Mark. Many can be found in town, including Central Park!

The class was glad when the boat docked at Liberty Island. A man named Bill greeted them. "I'm Park Ranger Bill," he said. "Welcome to the Statue of Liberty, an important national landmark," said Bill.

"*Park ranger* and *landmark*. Nouns made up of two or more words. What are they called?" Nathan asked.

"**Compound** nouns," said Nicole.

"Can I take your photo?" Nathan asked Bill.

"Sure," Bill said.

Snap! A compound noun picture.

Bill told the history of the statue.
"Lady Liberty was a gift from the people of
France to the people of the United States to
represent the two nations' friendship. Her
skin is made of copper."

"Listen for **plural** nouns," whispered Mrs. Smith.

"She welcomes people to our country," said Bill. "Her crown and torch represent liberty and freedom to people around the world. Now, feel free to take photos!"

Nicole sat on a bench to think. Some nouns are easy to change from **singular** to plural. You just add an -*s* or an -*es*. *Photo* becomes *photos*. **Irregular nouns** are trickier. For some, you change the word, not just the ending. *Person* becomes *people*. Then there are nouns you can't make plural, like *air*, *courage*, and *traffic*. They're called noncount nouns.

"Poets have to think hard to keep track of all this!" she thought.

A flock of seagulls landed on the statue. "*Flock* is a **collective** noun," said Mrs. Smith. Collective nouns describe a group.

"Let's think of as many collective nouns as we can!" said Nathan.

"Herd," said Meena, who wore an elephant T-shirt.

"Bunch," said Sam, munching on grapes.

"Class!" everyone said.

Nathan peeked at Nicole's notepad.

A <u>flock</u> of seagulls came to see the statue of Lady Liberty.

"Nice rhyme!" Nathan said.

Bill raised his hand. "Let's climb up to the crown."

Inside the crown, the students looked around. "Since we can see the crown, it's a **concrete** noun," said Nicole. "Poets like concrete nouns."

"Concrete nouns are experienced by the five senses. Sight. Sound. Smell. Touch. Taste," said Mrs. Smith. "Speaking of taste, who wants a snack?"

Outside, the class ate ice cream cones. "I'm eating a concrete noun! I can taste, smell, touch, and see my ice cream cone!" said Nathan.

"It's also a compound noun. It's made with more than one word," Nicole said.

"What's the opposite of a concrete noun?" asked Meena.

"An **abstract** noun," said Nicole. "Poets love abstract nouns, too. They let you talk about special feelings and ideas."

Miss Gomez walked over with the rest of the class. "Who can think of an abstract noun?" she asked.

"Freedom," said Meena.

"Liberty," said Sam.

"Happiness," said Nicole, scribbling hard.

Abstract nouns cannot be seen.
Some are <u>liberty</u> and <u>beauty</u>.
You can't make them in a machine.
Think <u>happiness</u> and <u>duty</u>!

Nathan put down his camera. If you can't see an abstract noun, how can you take its photo? This must be Miss Gomez's noun mystery!

Miss Gomez raised her eyebrows. "Can anyone tell me how we can take a photo of an abstract noun?"

Suddenly, Nathan realized how to do it. The students raised their ice cream cones like torches. Nathan focused his camera.

"CHEESE!" they yelled happily.

Snap! Liberty. Freedom. Happiness. Nathan's best photo all day—a beautiful abstract noun photo.

Just then, something flew through the air. Nicole caught it. It was her hat.

"Nouns are amazing!" she shouted.

"The Statue of Liberty"
By Nicole

Lady Liberty stands proud and tall.
As a noun, she is proper.
She stands for freedom for us all.
And she's made of copper!

Know Your Nouns

We need at least one noun to make a sentence. Most sentences have two or more. In a sentence, nouns have different jobs. One job is to be the subject of the verb. Read this sentence: Nathan snaps photographs. *Nathan*, the noun, is the subject of the verb. He snaps. Nouns can also be objects of the verb. The other noun, *photographs*, is the direct object of the verb. The photographs are what are being snapped.

Some nouns are proper nouns. They name people, places, and things. These nouns begin with capital letters. Read this sentence: We're visiting the Statue of Liberty. *Statue of Liberty* is a proper noun. Now, read this sentence: We're visiting a statue. Here, *statue* is not a proper noun, so it is not capitalized.

Many plural nouns are easy to make. You just add an s to the singular noun. For nouns that end in *-s*, *-sh*, *-ch*, *-x*, or *-z*, you usually add an *-es*. If a noun ends in a consonant and *y*, change the *y* to *i* and add *-es*. For example, *candy* changes to *candies*. Add an *-s* to nouns that end in a vowel and a *y*.

Find each noun in these sentences. Is it singular or plural? Abstract or concrete? Proper or common? Is it a collective or possessive noun? Take your time! Remember, nouns can be more than one of these types.

A French architect designed the famous statue.

Barges, tugboats, and fish share the harbor.

A troop of Girl Scouts visits the museum.

The torch is a symbol of liberty.

Emma Lazarus wrote a famous poem about the Statue of Liberty.

Writing Activity

Tooth, mouse, and man are irregular nouns. Now make them plural. Hint: You change the word, not just the ending. Some nouns don't change at all. Read this sentence: Sarah's sheep provide milk for her prize-winning cheese. Does Sarah have one sheep or more than one? Look for clues in the sentence.

Nouns such as *weather, sunshine*, and *honesty* don't have plural forms. They are called noncount nouns. Try thinking of as many noncount nouns as you can!

Now think of a place you like to visit. Make a list of plural nouns that relate to the place. Try to include some irregular nouns. Use a few noncount nouns, too. Then write a story about your trip. Try to use all the plural nouns you have listed. Have a fantastic trip!

Glossary

abstract: relating to an idea or quality that is not a person, place, or thing.

collective: naming a group of things or people.

compound: made up of more than one thing joined together.

concrete: naming a real person, place, or thing.

irregular nouns: nouns that undergo a major change when you make them plural, rather than just changing the endings.

plural: more than one of something.

possessive: showing ownership.

singular: one of something.

For More Information

Books

Cleary, Brian P. *Feet and Puppies, Thieves and Guppies: What Are Irregular Plurals?* (Words Are Categorical). Minneapolis, MN: Millbrook Press, 2014.

Time for Kids Editors. *TIME for Kids Grammar Rules!* New York: Time for Kids, 2013.

Websites

Proper Nouns
http://www.k12reader.com/term/proper-nouns
Learn more about different kinds of proper nouns at this website.

Nouns: Mrs. Warner's Fourth Grade Classroom
http://mrswarnerarlington.weebly.com/nouns.html
This website has links to games and videos about nouns.

About the Author

Ann Malaspina likes to write poems and take photographs of interesting places. She also enjoys writing books for children.